AF432404

Raindrops on Still Water

Poems for Practice

Tendo

Raindrops on Still Water
Poems for Practice

Revised and Expanded Edition, June 2026
First Edition June 2021
Copyright © 2026 by Robert j Kirkpatrick

Dream Mountain Press
6499 Wahl Rd.
Freeland WA 98249

All Rights Reserved.

ISBN-13: 979-8-234-03076-4

Cover photograph by Robert j Kirkpatrick

First Printing June 2026
10 9 8 7 6 5 4 3 2 1

Excerpts from **Dewdrops on Stinging Nettles**: *A Companion for Practice* used by permission of the author.

DreamMountain.org

Raindrops on Still Water

Poems for Practice

Preface

There are things that can be expressed through poetry that we can't convey in any other way. The manner in which people, events, scenery, and circumstances affects us, captivates us, and makes us feel is often best communicated in verse. Poems can delight us, tickle our fancy, or capture our melancholy, and thus are able to express sentiments that elude mere description. Verse can gesture toward the ineffable in ways that convey some sense of the infinite. But there is another aspect of poetry, one that relies on how our minds work, what our brains delight in, and that is to act as a catalyst, to activate our imagination and generate a creative and unique response in each reader.

I first came to understand this, and this understanding was in its own way a flash of insight, at a point during my long love affair with haiku. Traditional haiku, which has a lot more strictures than contemporary, at least contemporary western, culture ascribes to it, can do a lot in its minimalist form. But I found that the poems that resonated most powerfully were those that seemed to activate something in me, like that satisfying 'click' when you find where a piece in a puzzle fits in.

What that activation turned out to be was an element of the poem designed to take advantage of the mind of the reader to complete the image being sketched out in words. The way this typically works in haiku is the first two lines of the poem evoke a specific image, while the third line would present something that doesn't seem to quite fit. Not necessarily contradictory, but incongruous. Orthogonal. Our brains would then work to make this disparity fit in, to connect the dots, to tell the rest of the story. Thus for the poem to be 'complete' it depends upon the reader; the words on the page are insufficient to convey its intention. The result of this is that the 'completed' poem would be unique to each person. The poet would relinquish the control of painting a specific picture in lieu of this much more powerful activation that occurs in the mind of the reader. In effect the words of the poet acts as a catalyst to generate the actual poem—unique to each reader— which exists only in the mind of the reader.

Those who practice, that is engage in the investigation of *what is true*, and, *how then do we live*, have an instinctive mistrust of words and language, as they, by their very nature, reify the self. Language divides everything into subject and object, inherently conceptualizing by placing everything into neat and tidy boxes and attaching labels that surely are not the thing indicated. And yet, language is what we have to share the truths and practice with others, who are not yet beyond such conceptualizations. With practice one can learn how words can be used in a subtle way that elides much of the discriminatory modality inherent in most speech. Used skillfully words can be used to push past self-oriented thinking and beyond such conceptualizations. Our brains' natural desire to resolve contradictions can be utilized to facilitate this.

When I put together this skillful use of words and the way that disparate imagery in minimalist poetry acted as a catalyst upon the reader, the first inklings of Raindrops arose. How minimalist can poems become and still engender this effect? To what ends can they be used for practice? With experimentation I settled on four words. I found four-word poems work well as a way to occupy our conceptual minds as we engaged in the cultivation of *openness* or as an indirect method of investigation into *contradiction*.

Over the ensuing years I wrote many Raindrops—once you are in the zone they come quickly and effortlessly (see **Composing Raindrops** for the theory and practice of writing your own). When I published the initial version of **Dewdrops on Stinging Nettles**: *A Companion for Practice*, my book of Dream Mountain practices, I included instructions on using Raindrops as a component of one's practice as well as a generous selection of the poems. These were always intended to be their own book, a book of ultra-minimalist poems, but also a book for practice. This is that book, a living text that has space for the readers own poems as well as the ability to include more poems in subsequent editions.

—

This book is divided into two parts. The first section contains explanatory material, practice methodology and instructions on writing your own Raindrops. Throughout this first part, words that are in italics reference practices of the Dream Mountain Way. The **Notes** at the end of this section contain extracts from **Dewdrops on Stinging Nettles:** *A Companion for Practice* elucidating these various terms and techniques. Raindrops, as a practice, are another method that one can engage in, one that works holistically with the body of practices found in that book.

The second part is the main body of the book: a collection of three hundred Raindrops written over the past decade.

Tendo
Tahoma Zen Monastery
April 2026

Contents

Poems for Practice

Poems for Practice

Words have always failed to get at what is true; any attempt to capture *reality as is*, in something as limited as language, always fails. Language is not only incapable of expressing the infinite, it also inherently divides the world into subject and object. Even languages that aren't so strongly oriented in this way subtly reinforce the separation of the speaker and the listener. Yet words are how we can communicate the means of investigation into what is true.

Poetry has always been the most effective means of using language to gesture toward the ineffable. Through the spare use of words, leaning heavily on allusion, metaphor and abstraction it can give us a sense of things beyond our ken. We are familiar with this from poems that attempt to communicate singular experience, emotions and relationships.

There is also a tradition of poetry, often of a quite minimal nature, that grapples with the infinite. Utilizing open-ended metaphors, or comparisons to that which is already well beyond our grasp, it opens us up to these greater possibilities. One method for this is to engage our imagination to reconcile seeming opposites, to force us into a direct confrontation with contradiction. This is most effectively done with poems of just a handful of words deployed with subtlety and grace such that we don't dismiss it as a trick or an affectation, instead responding with wonder and delight.

When we move through the world without expectations, we see everything with fresh eyes, with a sense of wonder. It is this sense of wonder that makes every experience fresh, dynamic and ultimately joyful. This is an integral aspect of our experience, one that arises from our deepest nature. Our minds delight in solving puzzles at such a deep level that resolving a seeming contradiction brings us a fundamental, and boundless, delight.

Raindrops are a particularly minimal form of poetry that leans into all of these modalities. They eschew the inherent division of subject and object by not utilizing pronouns, in fact abandoning a clearly defined subject entirely. Connecting tissue, those parts of speech that divide, are let go and instead there is simply phenomena. It may utilize a single descriptive trait, but even then it is unclear how it relates. Some Raindrops may be only nouns, or only adjectives, perhaps with one verb that isn't clearly connected to any other word.

This structure leans on the reader's imagination to paint any sort of picture. But more essentially it takes advantage of that delight we take in solving puzzles. We can read, or say to ourselves, the four words of a Raindrop while walking, or gazing, as we carry on with whatever practice method or task we are engaged with. Behind the scenes our brains leap into gear, working to figure out these words, grappling with the contradiction. *What is the connection? What does it mean? What image is being painted?* Our minds must know, and thus, in the background, wrestle with it. This occupies the conceptual mind, so concerned with language, with naming, with reifying its separateness, allowing our attention to remain with *what is.*

This is a method of practice that synergistically works with any non-language based practice. It allows us to remain in awareness without expending effort, without engaging the will. It leverages the way our minds function, for the benefit of awakening to *reality as is.*

Practicing with Raindrops

When a single raindrop falls into a mirror-calm pool, subtle ripples texture the surface. We utilize this in questioning or investigating contradiction, casting words into the still pool of our minds and gazing at the ripples that emanate.

Raindrops are words used directly in their most bare and unadorned form—a poem, pared down to incompleteness. They utilize the still pool to resonate beyond the abstractions of words, beyond what they point at, beyond all conceptual thinking, beyond the self. When we are open and the still pool is truly mirror-calm, empty to such a depth that there are no distinctions between inner and outer, the subtle ripples reveal what is in this empty mirroring of things as they are. Working with Raindrops as a practice can also deepen the still pool, bringing us to this place of empty awareness where the depths are bottomless.

The practice is, as always, simple. Just be with an environment—inside, out of doors, walking, in an interstitial space, in stillness—with this book in your hands. We ground ourselves in our body, and open ourselves to the silence. We allow our thoughts to settle, *cultivating the still pool.* At an opportune moment, a moment that will arise naturally, we open the book to a random page and place our gaze upon one of the three Raindrops on the page, letting it drop into the still pool. Closing the book, perhaps closing our eyes, we wait for the ripples to come to shore, revealing the depths of the still pool, probing the unconscious, stirring up what it will.

In this practice, openness is essential. It is not a search for words that we have an affinity with, or that resonate in some way. Indeed, it is those words that may seem the most dissociative, the most incongruous, the most challenging, the most indirect, the most uncomfortable, the most devoid of meaning, that can be what current conditions demand. Equally, those words that do resonate, are in tune with current emotional undercurrents, conditional patterns, wider practices, mental states, or are found inspiring, insightful, and complementary might be what is currently required. We just take the Raindrop presented and engage with it beyond discrimination, beyond choice, beyond desire and ultimately beyond self.

We also use Raindrops in conjunction with other practices as a method to occupy our conceptual minds, leading to a more receptive, open state. In this modality as we set out on a walk, engage in gazing practices, or stillness sitting, and we use the process described above to randomly select a Raindrop. We read it through several times and then carry on with the practice. We simply let it percolate in the background, our brains grappling with it. The conceptual mind desires to resolve it and this occupies it without engaging the self. In this way we remain less distracted by thoughts and more open to the practice we are working with. As needed we can recite the poem to ourselves. Not to cut off thought, but as a periodic redirection of our conceptual minds.

There is a natural affinity in working with Raindrops out of doors, but they can be used in any environment and in any situation. Used in conjunction with the gazing practices, they can bring that probing uncertainty into a course of practice. This is working with not-knowing from a different angle than questioning or contradiction. This is more subtle, more turning words against themselves, and letting them do the work entirely. It does not engage will, effort, or the self. Indeed, they undercut the self, relying only on the still pool, on openness itself. Even when the still pool is choppy, they can be dropped in. This can calm down scattered, discriminatory thinking and settle us into a more and more still, open awareness.

Composing Raindrops

When working with Raindrops it is the negative space that they contain, their very ambiguity, that is their essential nature. This nature is entwined with their functioning and depends on the reader for activation. They are incomplete by nature; they are essentially empty. Their functioning is to generate in the reader the imagery that brings them to full fruition. Their power lies in the reality that this imagery will be unique to each reader and thus more impactful than any constructed image.

When composing Raindrops it is vital to work from this understanding. They are, in essence, imagistic, relying much more upon sights, sounds, and impressions than ideas, emotions, language, or turns of phrase. The mind 'connects the dots', as it were, and thus the 'dots' must be distant, yet connectable. The use of just nouns and adjectives is a way to achieve this. Yet verbs can be brought to play, which may bring some of these 'dots' closer together, shorten the distance between connections or, to put it another way, set a direction for the reader's mind to wander. But a light touch is vital. Being too on the nose, holding the reader by the hand, or trying to impose a specific vision–these lead to dead, inactive poems unable to spark the imagination of the reader.

When Raindrops are used for practice they occupy the conceptual mind, which delights in making connections, solving puzzles and exercising the imagination. The activities of the mind are not controlled by the self, as much as it may insist that is so. The response of the mind when encountering a Raindrop is to engender these connections, to resolve the incongruity. The way they work in practice, depends upon this behavior of the mind. This is why Raindrops are four words —this is something the mind will work on in the background. A longer poem, even one similarly minimalistic such as haiku, inspires the self to try to relate itself to the poem. The abstract, ultra-minimal nature of Raindrops bypasses this tendency, but not the tendency of the mind to try to connect the dots.

Taking into account all these considerations guides us in the most natural and effective way in composing Raindrops. With natural imagery being the most effective, it is thus most efficacious to compose these out of doors. Engage in a practice such as *walking* or *stillness sitting* while out of doors. Everything that falls upon our gaze is a natural subject. We can see or hear or feel attributes of these subjects. Are the clouds tattered like a torn veil? Are the ferns glistening green with morning dew? Do the waves crash with exuberance? We take these elements, one or more objects and one or more attributes and simply lay them out two words above two words. In this way we have constructed a Raindrop.

When composing Raindrops following this methodology we can iterate on the poem. That is we may take one subject and over multiple poems focus on specific attributes or spin connections with varying subjects. We can explore different words that catch at these attributes, but have a different valence to them. Alternatively we may substitute different objects leaving the rest of the poem intact. Attributes, such as colors that may describe water, sky, foliage, landscapes and so on, can be used in lieu of these objects. The mind will make the connections, each in their own way. In this the power and flexibility of the poems unfold.

When out *walking* we stay with the practice, but if we find ourselves caught on words, we deploy a Raindrop. We might generate one on the spot using what we see or hear. Then we stay with the practice and let the mind grapple with it. But then on a break, perhaps for lunch, or to rest, we pull out a handy note-taking implement and record the Raindrop and all the iterations that come to mind. When we are open to the process they are generated quickly. You cannot have enough Raindrops, for when we use our own it is essential that the initial connections we have made be forgotten. With a vast collection of Raindrops this is all but assured.

The many hundreds of Raindrops in this book will serve admirably as they are all new to the reader. But there is also a generous quantity of empty pages at the end of the collection to add your own. Over time these will just be another set of words for your mind to grapple with allowing you to *focus* on the method you are engaged in thus sustaining *continuous practice*.

How to Use this Book

When you are practicing, in any circumstance or situation, and you are bedeviled by conceptual thinking, this is a time to deploy Raindrops. We use them similarly to how we use *indirect probing* which is that we read the phrase when thoughts are prevalent and then we return our gaze to our method and let the mind work on it in the background. This is fully explored in **Practicing With Raindrops**. Here we will offer suggestions on how to make the selection of a particular Raindrop to engage with.

It is imperative that preferences are abandoned and not allowed to guide one in selecting the Raindrop to work with. If we choose one that we 'like' or feel 'resonates' with us, then that will engage the self which will gladly take on the project. Instead, we must randomly select the Raindrop to work with, thus taking our biases out of the loop. The most straightforward method is to simply flip pages in the book and then stab our finger into the open page at the top, middle or bottom of the page. The text is laid out with three Raindrops per page and this method will direct us to one to work with. Even if we find we lean toward the top, bottom or middle, it won't make much difference (though we should attempt to subvert these tendencies as much as we can).

If we choose to eliminate any preferences, there are ways to randomize our choices. Throwing a six-sided die and having 1 & 2 be the top poem, 3 & 4 the middle poem and 5 & 6 the bottom poem is one option. Other methods such as flipping coins, drawing straws and so on can be adapted.

Likewise we can use a more random method for selecting the page of the book, since flipping pages does favor the middle of the book. If you are using an electronic version of the book you will have to use a random page selection method and then the electronic readers 'go to page' function. Multiple dice can be used, or pulling numbers out of a hat. Additionally there are numerous applications that one can use to generate a random number within a range, simply setting it to the first and last page of the text. This also could be used for the top, middle and bottom poem selection.

Whatever method we utilize to select the poem, we stick with the selection disregarding our likes and dislikes. Those that don't seem to 'harmonize' will all the more occupy the mind. We then read it through a number of times until we have it internalized and then put the book away and continue on with our practice.

Notes

In this section we offer extracts from **Dewdrops on Stinging Nettles**: *A Companion for Practice* on various methods that are referenced in the prefatory material. Raindrops, as a practice, engage synergistically with this body of practices helping us to put down distractions, occupying the conceptual mind and thus leading us ever deeper. Please see Dewdrops on Stinging Nettles for more on these practices and the Dream Mountain Way.

All extracts used by permission.

Dewdrops on Stinging Nettles:
A Companion for Practice
By Tendo
Dream Mountain Press, 2025
ISBN: 979-8-218-60813-2

Preface

Openness

Openness is our natural condition, a condition that the barrier of the self has created an illusory separation from. Openness can't be forced; we must ease into it naturally. We become increasingly open by cultivating the still pool and settling into awareness of our entire bodies. Then we can open up further by listening, letting sounds in without discrimination, without placing attention on them. This brings our sense of awareness beyond ourselves. (p. 40)

Contradiction

The method of working with contradiction is in utilizing questions, prompts, and dialogs, that elude conceptualization, that have no "answer" or "solution" that can be puzzled out, or arrived at by thinking. This is the inherent nature of contradiction: to resolve the contradiction we have, to abandon critical processes, and let go of conceptualization. (p. 96)

Dream Mountain Way

The Dream Mountain Way is an approach to deeply committed practice within the circumstances of this world. The Dream Mountain Way is to make our very lives a full-time training environment. Oriented around the close observation of natural processes, these practices point toward every sense, every thought, every moment as a method of direct practice

Poems for Practice

Walking
We walk out in the woods, across fields, in mountains, on the beach, in the landscape. As we walk, our gaze takes in what comes, all the forms shining within. We walk in our bodies, from the abdomen, breathing naturally. We pause and gaze out in the distance. If birds fly across our gaze, we hold them in our minds, no separation. If the tops of the trees sway, they sway in our minds. Sunlight dances on water, dragonflies dart through our field of view. We let all of these reflect in the deep still pool of our minds. (p. 81)

Gazing
In the gazing practices, we engage with our surroundings such that we don't project ourselves into the world. Instead, we see what is in our sensory field as shining into us. The practice of gazing is being fully open to where attention has been placed. We stay with the subject of attention without labeling, discriminating or commenting upon it. If such language arises, we let it naturally pour away. We simply are open to what is in the field of view. We allow this openness to persist

for a sustained duration. Time, which is inextricable from thought, will flow away, as thoughts flow away. As attention releases, awareness opens up. We let this naturally occur. Very gently, seamlessly gazing, this widens from dwelling upon our field of view into an open awareness. (p. 51)

Practicing with Raindrops

The Still Pool

Becoming like a perfectly still pool—reflecting everything and nothing, no distinction between interior and exterior—this is the nature of this practice. There are numerous ways into this modality: following the breath, relaxing into awareness, intensive investigation and the myriad gazing practices. This orientation is one of naturalness: being in our body, following its lead, flowing effortlessly without engaging the self. The question of effort is a vital one. Whenever there is effort, the will is engaged and the will is the functioning of the self. But we can use effort to establish a practice, over time relaxing the use of self-directed effort, and becoming ever more natural. (p. 29)

Empty Awareness

When we are rooted in our direct experience, our internal monologue falls away and we are just operating as awareness. Awareness is the functioning of reality as is. This is being in tune with original nature–simply pure awareness expressing itself through our provisional forms, through our bodies. When our sense of identity is rooted in our original nature, this is empty awareness. Normally, our identity is centered in a sense of self, which is an amalgam of memories, feelings, and conditioning. When we are able to see through our conditioning and let go of it, this sense of the separate self is seen as fundamentally empty. Empty awareness is what remains. (p. 137)

Writing Raindrops

Stillness Sitting

Stillness-sitting, in all its diverse forms, is a core method for investigation. Stillness in our body is reflected in our minds and thus is a prerequisite for sustained practice. Stability is essential and it is the basis of posture, but posture is not the practice; it is simply a tool we use in order to enhance investigation. In the Dream Mountain Way, we sit anywhere… Even sitting is not essential. We can stand still and engage in many of these practices, and when walking, we are not separate from stillness. Thus as we consider more formal approaches, note the essence and how that can be manifested in any situation. (p. 31)

Focus

It is vital to be able to place our awareness, to naturally let energy flow to a single point, concentrating our scattered minds. Through practice, we can develop this skill which is the crux of so many methods. The ability to focus our awareness upon an object, be it in the environment, in our bodies or in our mind, is essential to engage in many practices. But it also is a practice in and of itself. A focused mind is not filled with scattered thoughts, and ultimately is empty of a sense of self. (p. 37)

Continuous Practice

The Dream Mountain Way is a pragmatic, hands-on approach to continuous practice. In our daily lives, on pilgrimage, in solitude, on retreat, amidst all activity–in every circumstance, everything is an opportunity for practice. We must strive to not limit ourselves to any particular modality. It is the circumstances that arise in every domain that we must respond to and that is the most essential practice. We take every opportunity, every moment, as a good friend, pointing at the way, illuminating where there is work to be done, endlessly murmuring "not yet", "not yet." (p. 115)

How To Use This Book

Indirect Probing

With indirect probing, we load our minds with the question and let it be worked on in our subconscious. Throughout the day, we may ask the question to keep it active, but the process is more background. Our subconscious strives to solve the question, just as we may wake up from sleep with the answer to a problem from our daily activities. With these questions having no answer, the contradiction generates increasing uncertainty, ultimately confounding the conceptual mind. Over time the conceptual mind begins to break down, revealing its constructed and illusory nature. If at times an answer seems to arise, perhaps on waking, perhaps in a flash of intuition, then we question that. Any answer becomes our next question until there are no questions left, the self falling away. (p. 91)

Raindrops

slate sky
open eyes

—

green slowly
turning brown

—

sitting falling
rain bell

snow falling
green mountains

—

rushing water
scattered moonlight

—

cloud mountain
no path

flowing water
broken reflections

—

dark clouds
mountain snow

—

sitting watching
blowing wind

cloud fading
blue skies

—

tree note
green flash

—

empty path
green hills

one cloud
empty mirror

—

white clouds
falling leaves

—

empty sky
ringing bell

one cloud
blue mirror

—

red cloud
sea reflection

—

blue skies
dew drops

grass blade
one drop

—

blue sky
no clouds

—

one cloud
absent mind

walking pursued
red dragonflies

—

heaven path
unbounded effort

—

sitting still
birds return

distant clouds
hills grey-green

—

jagged ridge
deep green

—

grey sky
bright clouds

warm south
wind ceases

—

rocks ants
everywhere weeds

—

grey above
grey below

dead branch
wandering ants

—

chittering cawing
buzzing flowing

—

shaking leaves
floating free

ripple blue-white
clouds shadows

—

green leaves
blowing wind

—

jagged water
rain drop

rock body
trees ants

—

grey space
between leaves

—

chopped small
peaks waves

spring rain
wind stir

—

waves again
again waves

—

impossible grey
shapes grey

green surrounds
grey peaks

—

confused tangles
green grey

—

wind stirs
through mind

rocks water
see through

—

distant rain
mind empty

—

far near
black clouds

glowing clouds
blue edges

—

nail moon
sail shadow

—

dream feather
fall water

gone empty
branches tangle

—

calm water
feather falling

—

fall water
feather spiral

tangled branches
blue space

—

entangled branches
inner pattern

—

breath ground
negative space

turquoise waters
softly drifting

—

in between
sudden now

—

look through
empty branches

look through
entangled space

—

look through
negative space

—

summer trees
lone pinecone

hovering flies
gentle breeze

—

just this
empty space

—

open gaze
entangles gaps

through trees
endless waves

—

filtered light
shadow space

—

surround birds
patterns chirping

grey waters
grey skies

—

rock ocean
tree sand

—

setting boiling
ocean sun

threads fall
gaze through

—

no thing
remains so

—

wait open
let go

blue clouds
white gone

—

bright cloud
empty sky

—

light filtered
trees green

shale moss
splintered mist

—

pale moss
splintered sky

—

clouds scrub
peaks breeze

sky shadows
broken clouds

—

cloud walking
green roots

—

white walking
green roots

walking pursued
by dragonflies

—

white winds
cold pine

—

white winds
cold flowers

man ocean
walking gone

—

fog horn
surf warmth

—

obscured sand
waves fog

obscured sand
ripples fog

—

obscured birds
tidelands fog

—

obscured birds
wheeling fog

shadow fog
rushing sand

—

waiting tide
white trees

—

birds blue
surf cry

cone leaf
disintegrating blue

—

come leaf
withered tree

—

come withered
leaves stump

butterfly vivid
plant green

—

withered sky
blue tree

—

grey green
blue white

wobbly sun
breeze falling

—

failing sun
diffused crow

—

time sun
dim swaying

moon gulls
haze shadow

—

moon birds
cry mist

—

moon mist
sans waves

grey line
ocean sky

—

clouds ocean
no difference

—

ocean seal
boundless reflection

overlapping mirror
ocean seal

—

all things
stamped brightness

—

bright mirror
ocean seal

clouds ocean
moon seal

—

clouds ocean
not two

—

blue clouds
white gone

bright clouds
empty sky

—

gone empty
branches temple

—

wood heart
call birds

right clouds
gone empty

—

grey sky
bright clouds

—

in between
sudden now

pinecone past
open gaps

—

bird fading
hole flutter

—

waiting waiting
chirping chirping

past pinecone
gaze through

—

dragonfly gone
falling leaves

—

rough bark
fly toward

wispy beach
roaring clouds

—

crinkled peak
ice fade

—

wind rock
ice peril

white clouds
grey peaks

—

flowing ice
blowing clouds

—

wind rock
water clouds

clouds roiling
ridge mind

—

sun outcropping
mountain wind

—

beyond mountains
blowing words

breaking mountains
sitting forgetting

—

fractal clouds
endless peaks

—

beyond mountains
thought mountains

nothing rock
what remains

—

red dragonfly
good year

—

turquoise water
sun inside

red dragonfly
grass fire

—

grass crystal
no dragonfly

—

known empty
green waiting

sun wakes
dragonfly gone

—

green trees
absent spaces

—

moonlight waters
owls calling

nothing knowing
red dragonfly

—

birds distance
quiet fog

—

empty knowing
empty earth

good year
dragonflies look

—

owls call
no knowing

—

obscure far
binding away

looking deep
red dragonfly

—

moonlit owls
calling waters

—

moss hazy
sky pillows

look deeper
deeper still

—

no shadow
only clouds

—

no shadow
no clouds

gliding crow
look look

—

empty shadow
no clouds

—

empty shadow
empty clouds

sky veins
open mind

—

weeds moss
trees absence

—

sharp rocky
moss seat

blowing clouds
chirping buzzing

—

small priority
green inside

—

hanging moss
distant bell

turquoise waves
white birds

—

inside wind
wailing waves

—

empty shadow
no kings

look down
white waves

—

inside wind
rolling waves

—

far mountains
rocky snow

weather reveals
inside patterns

—

rippling patterns
inside waters

—

absent tracings
sky-blue seas

bluff rock
water trees

—

nothing weaker
ripples trailing

—

white dots
dark blue

veins twists
grey fading

—

fading blue
weather path

—

inner pattern
ripples clouds

cold wind
rippled water

—

vast horizon
freezing winds

—

structured space
clouds tear

horizon kelp
rock bluff

—

pattern space
cloud path

—

steep waves
drifting forget

inside peaks
fog blanket

—

rolling clouds
wind chill

—

outsider sail
no pattern

shrouds fail
reaching hiss

—

thin line
obscured flying

—

black space
lighter rippled

barnacle blue
empty dark

—

three birds
turn clouds

—

drifting alone
pounding waves

pebbled skin
tearing across

—

no light
no layers

—

filtered grey
seeing through

washed layers
mountain clouds

—

blurred clouds
mountain rain

—

dark ship
distant blue

broken blue
far thought

—

tattered waves
broken rain

—

waves fade
sky road

soft layers
fade sky

—

pebble mounds
diffused footprints

—

tattered blue
soft fatigue

broken water
round rock

—

root hair
rock bed

—

fading clouds
creeping hills

shore path
rocky golden

—

sand driftwood
cold breeze

—

golden hue
sitting shrubs

rocky path
golden shore

—

far rushing
warmth clouds

—

real point
faraway winds

floating trees
fallen clouds

—

drifting waiting
clouds waiting

—

golden hue
sitting shrubs

idle clouds
sitting wall

—

sun clouds
not yet

—

far off
surf bluffs

into shadow
cold sleep

—

deeper tears
deeper rock

—

between branches
empty absence

into shadow
cold sun

—

deep deep
look look

—

far off
tangled clouds

tangled clouds
water shadow

—

faraway tears
tangled shadow

—

not far
is it

three blue
yellow dragonflies

—

bunched clouds
dappled white

—

far away
it is

soft breeze
shelling water

—

green hills
white patch

—

blue soft
green words

over blue
under blue

—

line water
lime clouds

—

horizon bunched
clouds ants

wisps wheeling
ridge patterning

—

inner skin
outer mind

—

sky above
reflecting below

blue white
green blue

—

empty black
blue cutout

—

stone seat
pretext flies

no seat
protect flies

—

snow peaks
deep cutout

—

deep turquoise
deep cutoff

jagged rocks
snow streaks

—

frozen lake
falling water

—

ice creaks
mountains rushing

breeze play
sun mountains

—

drink snow
rock feat

—

sweat unwind
jagged edge

hard scramble
blue eye

—

shattered eyes
overlaid light

—

snow ledge
almost gone

trees barren
snow burden

—

rocks ants
snow barren

—

threads clouds
white awake

leaves barren
snow breeze

—

leaves gust
fallen clouds

—

leaves green
falling brown

leaf breeze
falling clouds

—

gaps white
no gaps

—

golden shaking
calling brambles

angles wind
dropping tangled

—

gaps white
shaking swing

—

golden shakings
calling branches

stop golden
hover grass

—

waning waiting
singing dreaming

—

no song
left way

dragonfly gaps
no space

—

grass waiting
brown space

—

waiting call
end butterfly

dragonfly scattered
no gaps

—

ending withered
flying falling

—

look hover
upon distance

grass waiting
brown gaps

—

ending grass
dragging leaves

—

distant ending
little clear

now fall
hole unitary

—

sitting grass
elbow time

—

shaking light
this framing

now fall
no holes

—

distant endings
all clear

—

no fall
gap waiting

stillness fan
silence focus

—

finding this
nothing time

—

roaring gap
stay inside

many waiting
just see

—

please all
empty remember

—

no ending
everything clear